Teotokos

A NEW CREATION

Teotokos
A NEW CREATION

JOSEPH M

LitPrime
"Your story is our priority"

LitPrime Solutions
21250 Hawthorne Blvd
Suite 500, Torrance, CA 90503
www.litprime.com
Phone: 1-800-981-9893

Published by LitPrime Solutions   06/15/2022

ISBN: 978-1-955944-83-0(sc)
ISBN: 978-1-955944-84-7(e)

Library of Congress Control Number: 2022907775

The Message

By
Joseph Moctezuma Rivera

THE MERCY OF KNOWLEDGE

God gives a secret knowledge of Him to each being in existence in accordance to his or her situation, suffereing and victimazation of his or her life

God does not let anyone live a life of suffering, despairbgd and loneliness unless they get a secret knowledge of God only known by them in their despair

God is merciful by letting this poor, marginazed, and victimized, something about Him in their state of mind and reality which they live.

We live our lives unaware of ourselves, not knowing who we are, what we are, or why we are. Until we wake up and become conscious of ourselves, that when the suffering, despari, anxiety, angst of existence become evidence. By knowing ourselves we start to live a reality incomprehensible, obtused, obsurd and complex where our sense of balance and direction becomes upside down and we see life but a joke and death is real.

Yet even with this unbearable reality, God gives a wonderful gift of knowing something about Himself within the confines of sanity. We still know even when we are crazy for God is master of the dead and the livng the sane and the insane . The now and forever,

Don't be afraid to received God knowledge with in your Reality

IMMACULATE CONCEPTION

Holy Mother, Mother of God
Christ Redeemed you in Perfect Preservation
Exempting you from sin, which befall all of us who falls from
Grace . that only Jesus in your womb would have done
Preserving you from the Fall
From Thee, God's reveal two natures in Jesus: Jesus can
redeemed the fallen and exempt the selected one like you
from sin, making you without stain of sin
The Purity of your heart is predestined from the beginning
Immaculate Conception not from your parents
But from the womb by which you carry God Himself.
Mary of absolute Purity, pray for us the sinners without
Grace.
Mary the second Eve, bring us to paradise again
You are the Tabernacle exempt from defilement and
corruption on which we offer God our sacrifice
Immaculate Conception, most complete Sanctity. Perfect
justice do not let us be deceived by the serpent
Immacculate Conception, there is immunity in Heaven against
sin and you are the carrier of that vaccine

THE IMMACULATE CONCEPTION

The angel announcement

When the Arc Angel Saint Gabriel said to the Virgen Mary: "Blessed Mary full of Grace" God is with Thee "was not because she was full of Grace in her, but it was due to the life trayectory of her Holy and Blessed Existence by which she had to endure and suffered through the many trials and tribulations that befall of one of truly gracious nature"

From her Immaculate Conception, to the overcoming of the Holy Spirit and the Birth of our Saviour, through the Innormous suffering of the Passion, Cruxificcion and Ressurrectio of our Lord and finally the Glorious Accesscion of our Lord and Hers to heaven

It was an annoucement of the Past, future and Present: a prophecy fulfill e dint he past as well in the present

The Grace that we notice her is a linear Grace. Up to the death of her beloved son and beyond this horrendous happening, Mary was full of Grace. She was a living prophecy

Pope Pious IX had the vision that the Virgen Grace does not start at any point of her continous line of life so that it will increase or decrease in Grace. IT was a prophecy of Grace made in stone. The Gift of Grace of God was a complete gift from the inception to the Aseccension into Heaven

And because of this She was without sin or "Stain" of Sin.,

In 1854 Pope Pious IX announced this to the world the feast of our Immaculate Conception

In page 492 of the Catholic Cathequism reads that our Virgen Mary was redeemed of such a manner due to the merits of her son Jesus.

The Virgen was without sin ! in this premise we based everthing else of the virgin! For example : the price that we pay for sin is death . but if our Lady is without sin, She won't have to die, becaue She is without sin, so in conclusion is that the Virgen won't die but is taken into heaven like Enoch, Elijah, the Virgen did not die but was taken into heaven for two very strong reasons: she is without sin and She believed in lher Son: does it say in the Bible on the Gospel of John: he that believes in Jesus while still alive, won't die

The Secret of Grace

La Gracia es la forma que Dios anticipa a salvar al
humano que todavia no a nacido a la Vida eternal
Viene siendo la extension de la cual Dios salva al
Humano

Grace is the way by which God anticipates in saving
humanity that is not born yet to eternal life.

It is how God extends himself to save us. S

LET IT BE

In honor of our Virgen Mary,
Immaculate Conception

Let me be not the one who chooses oh Lord, but the one
chosen by your Grace

Because there is no greater life than the one received,
because everything is new in her.

Let me be the one selected to your Kingdom, not the
kingdom chosen by me

Do not give me the freedom to choose, but the freedom
of being chosen

Let me be the one found first God, so I can be able to
seek you Lord

The road is made by walking it, your Holy Spirit walks in
my being before I am aware of it

You love me first before I began to love you Lord, from
my mother's womb I you call me for your Holy Work

You have selected, me first no I Thee, God hidden in me

TEOTOKOS

The great privilege of being selected to be Immaculate
since my concepcion

The great Miracle of being saved for Eternal Life

I arrived to your Home oh Lord without merit, but with
the privilege of Grace to be chosen by the highest to be
for you oh God.

Let me be selected from the beginning, by you not by
me so I can end in Thee.

Let things find me before I find them, so if I find them is
by Grace and not by merit

Love choose me, not I selected love

It was a Gift my life, gratuitiously given, without price
cost of purchase

I have the most beautiful, good and truthful because of
your Grace oh Lord

Do not give me the need to choose, nor the virtue of
haven chosen

Do not give me the magic of control, but the miracle of
the given
Do not give me the blind fortune of chance but the
marked steps of your path

Do not give me the control of idolatry, but the aperture
of accepting all those things I cannot control

Knowing that your heaven is open do give without merit.

Surprise me with your 'Grace that is the most loved and awaited gift of my heart. Amen

I am your child, that is why I been chosen, so that you work is done in me amen

THE SECRET OF GRACE

The Queen of Heaven is like a Queen Bee in the honey comb, which we are all her sons and daughters in Spirit, in Grace and in Truth, and the honey we collect and sustain us is the Word of God that lead us to Eternal Life

His Sacred Word is in a field of flowers, disbursed in all the fields of creation, the flowers that live by the Light of Heavens above

We are Newborns, because we were not aborted by our mother when we were embrios not ready to be born, incubented in this material world, but when the time comes, we will be ready to be born to eternal and new life

In this embrio state, the devil try to kill us before being born of Truth Grace and Spirit. But our older Brother the First One of all the living, was born first out the Womb of our Holy Mother and He gave us the rite of passage to the New Life where there is no death

God wants us not to die y He live in constant diligence of us for the nine months of pregnancy in the earthly world as embrios

Heavenly Mother Queen of all the Living. From God comes the Love and from thou comes the new life in

Heaven . in this we can say we are part of our heavenly
Father (God)

Mother Mary, mother of God(Theotocos) pray for the
unborn in the hour of our birth amen

In apocalysis Chapter 12 there appears in heaven a
sign ; a pregnant woman ready to give birth appears
with a twelve stars crown and a Serpent appears trying
to devour the New Born

THE FIRST EVENGELAZATION

The Advent brings us the gifts of the Spirit and we
received them in our times and culture as talents
Our Lord Jesus Chinist expect us to use those
wonderful talents on evangelizing in the name of
the Father, the Son and the Holy Spirit to all
nations
The American continent is blessed with such
diversity of talents and gifts for evangelization

Th mother of the Redeemer has also been present
among the people of God in America from the very
begining of the New Evangelization, but in a
special Imanner from (53) when the apparition to
Juan Diego on the Tepeyac Hill, She, The Virgen
offered her maternal protection under the title of
Guadalupe to all the people of the American
Continent
Our Lady of Guadalupe : as the first evangelizer of
America and as the star of evangelization for the
third Millennium
Under many othe title is Mary venerated as
TEOTOKOS which means the mother of God
And mother of fall peoples in the different american
counties, when the faithful maanifest their
unmistakable membership in the Catholic Church
For this same reason, Pope John Paul 11
Gave Guadalupe the title Star of the New

15

Evangelization and also Star a the First
Evangelization in Palestine,2000 years ago

On the Great Jubilee, our Lady of Guadalupe will
be a model of conversion, communion and
solidarity for the Church in America, when all races
and people of different background conveyed and
manifest theirfruefaith in the Mother of God
The Spirit who transformed Mary into the first one
evangelized and the first evangelizer is the same
Spirit that abide in us today
In this Advent, revealing to us the American Virgen
Mary: Our Lady of Guadalupe

ACTS; 12:14

THE VIRGEN DIALOGUE

Narrator: On December 8, teo years after the conquest of Tenochtitlan, now Mexico City, a native called Juan Diego was walking across a hill called Tepeyac. He was going to Tlatelolco to attend catechism. Juan Diego was listening to the beautiful singing of the birds, when the Mother of God appeared.

The first apparition occurred, in a place that is now known as the "Capital del Cerrito", where the Blessed Virgin Mary talked to him in his language, nahuatl. She called him:

Virgin: Juanito, Juan Dieguito", the most of my sons". "my son the least", "my Little dear"
"My dear little son, I love you, I desire you to know who I am. I am the ever-Virgin Mary, Mother of the true God who gives life and maintains its existence. He created all things. He is in all places He is the Lord of Heaven and Earth. I desire a church in this place where you people my experience my compassion, All those who sincerely ask my help in their work and in their sorrows will know my Mother's Heart in this place. Here I will see their tears: I will console them and they will at peace. so run now to and tell the Bishop all that you have seen and heard.

SECOND APPARITION

Juan Diego: "My holy One, my Lady, I will do all you asked of me.
Narrator: After the bishop did not believed Juan Diego, Juan Diego directed himself to Tepeyac and as he approached the rocky hill, he clambered up the stony slope and found the Virgin Mary there.

Juan Diego: "Noble Lady, I obeyed your orders, but he did not believe me." I beg you to, Noble Lady to entrust your message to someone of importance, someone Well known and respected, so that your Wish Will be accomplished.

"For I am only a lowly peasant and you, my Lady, have sent me to a place where I have no standing. Forgive me if I have disappointed you for having failed in my mission.

Virgin Mary:" Listen to me, my dearest son, and understand that I have many servants and messengers whom I could charge with the delivery of my message. But it is altogether necessary that you should be the one to undertaken this mission and that it be through your mediation and assistance that my wish should be accomplished. I urge you to go to the Bishop again tomorrow and repeat to him that it is I in person the ever Virgin Mary, the Mother of God, who send you"

Juan Diego: "Holy Lady, I will not disappoint you. I will gladly go again at your command, even though once more may not be believed. Tomorrow towards sunset, I shall return here and give an account of the Bishop's respond.

Narrator: the Bishop requested a sign from the Virgin, and left to the Virgin what kind ofsign it would be.

THIRD APPARITION

Narrator: the Lady smiled at Juan Diego in full appreciation of his efforts.

Virgin Mary: that is very Well, my son, return here tomorrow and you will have the sign Bishop requested. Then he will believe and no longer doubt or suspect ofyou. "Marked my words well, my little son: I shall richly reward you for all the worry, work and trouble you have undertaken on my behalf. You may go home now. Tomorrow, I shall be waiting here for you.

FOURTH APPARITION

Narrator: next morning, Juan Diego's uncle was found and Juan Diego hurry to fetch a and forget about the meeting with the Virgin; When She appeared suddenly on his path, Juan Diego was shame and confused.

Virgin Mary: What is the matter my little son, where are you going.

Juan Diego: Noble Lady, it will grieve you to hear what I have to say: My uncle, your poor servant is very ill, I am hurrying to the church in Mexico City to call a priest to hear his confession give him the last rites. Please forgive me and be patient with me. I am not deceiving you. I promise to come here tomorrow with all haste.

Virgin Mary: "Listen let it penetrate your heart my dear son. "do not be troubled or weighed down with grief. Do not fear any illness or vexation, anxiety or pain. Am I not here who am your Mother? Are you not under my shadow and protection? Am I am not your fountain of life? Are you not in the folds of my mantle? In the crossing of my arm? Is there anything else you need? Do not let the illness of your uncle worry you because he is not going to die of his sickness. At this very moment he is cured.

Narrator: She directed Juan Diego to collect flowers on the top of the hill where she appeared for the first time. Juan Diego did as instructed and once he gatlwtâ€¢ed castelian roses and the heap to her, the Virgin Mary arranged the flowers with her hands.

Virgin Mary: my little son. These varied flowers are the sign, which you are to take to the Bishop. Tell him that in them he will recognize my will and that he must fulfill it. To the reveal the contents of your tilma until you are in his presence.

Juan Diego Nodded

Narrator: Juan Diego took the flowers to the Bishop and as unfolded the tilma. the image of the Virgin

Mary appeared embroidered by falling flowers on Juan Diego's tilma Once again the world was taught to believe.

Nican mopohua

THE NEW GENESIS

Thru the Grace of God, the woman being the creature of lowest status in Antiquity, She succeded in being the conduit of the God's Glory, making known to all times that God favors the humble and sincere in heart. The downthrodden, transforming them in the power and absolute Glory of God.

Since the time of Mary, Women had been degraded and subestimated delegating her a role of inferiority and without dignity. She has been reduced to a object of sale. a property without privilege or right. God took this lowely based vessel and made her the vehicle of salvation to all men.

God elevated this woman to be the author of her own liberation against the slavery and prej udicial conditions of the times. In the mother of God, our Virgen Mary we find the two human conditions: the marginalized woman of the society of her time. and of the woman I liberalized for the Glory of God.

In this condition, Mary represent the universal woman, being she the first woman that it is manifested the freedom from sin, for the benefit of men and woman of all times .

Bringing forth to the world the New Creation, not only the mother of salvation(thru Jesus) but the mother of the new Genesis and anouncing by this the New Humanity.

Thru the Grade of God, the mystery of Her Virginity symbolized the New Age, the prelude to a New Begining of a new World redemeed and Free from Sin.

Mary is the new Eve of the new Creation and mother of the New Humanity which obeys and reflect the Holiness of God.

Thru Cho First: Eve, came sin to the world. Thru Mary mother of God came the new purification of the World and the Holiness of men. The New Genesis requires an inversion of its own creation.

What does this mean, ? It means that we have reached the second level of creation: own perfection.

Every creation does not: start perfect. From inception, creation starts imperfect. but it perfects thru Grace to the second level to the new Genesis.

When the whole of Creation starts inverting, a new age of perfection arrives. But it comes with Mary .

Luke 1:26 - 38

UNCONDITIONAL LOVE OF MARY

MARY IS THE MOTHER OF A NEW FAMILY, ORIGINATED
WHEN JESUS SAID MARY AT THE FOOT OF THE CRUZ;
"WOMAN, THERE IS YOUR SON. SON THERE IS YOUR
MOTHER" THIS IS THE NEW FAMILY OF THOSE NEW
SONS BORN FROM BAVVISM, ORIGINATED BY FAITH.
THEREFORE WE CANNOT CALL OURSELVES BROTHERS
WITHOUT A MOTHER. BECAUSE THE LOVE OF A MOTHER
IS UNCONDITIONAL, WITHOUT LIMIT OR RESERVATIONS.
THE LOVE OF MARY AS MOTHER IS SIMILAR TO LOVE OF
GOD FOR ALL OF US AS SONS . THAT LOVE IS SO BEAUTIFUL
DEMONSTRATED EN THE PARABLE OF THE PRODIGAL SON.
IT IS A LOVE WITHOUT LIMIT. FORGIVENESS WITHOUT
RESERVATION.THIS IS THE LOVE OF THE MOTHER AND
OF MARY FOR US.

John 19:25-27

MARY, A SYMBOL OF YOUTH

HOW CAN THE YOUTH THEMSELVES WITH MOTHER OF GOD? A QUESTION THAT I HAVE ALWAYS ASKED IN TNIS ADVENT TO PREPARED LIKE SHE DID FOR THE COMING OF HER SON AND OF OUR SAVIOR.

THE FIRST THINK A SEE IS THAT SHE IS YOUNG, VERY YOUNG WHEN SHE WAS WITH CHILD, 12 TO 14 YEARS OF AGE. WHEN ONE SEES HER BEATIFUL FACE, SHE HAS A YOUNG FACE. SHE IS THE SYMBOL OF YOUTH IN HER HEART, MIND, SPIRIT AND BODY AND SOUL. THE SECOND MARIAN REALIZATION IS THAT GOD RESERVE HIS MOST POTENT MIRACLE FOR THE YOUNG. BECAUSE IT WAS THROUGH A YOUNG MAIDEN THAT SALVATION WOULD COME TO A OLD SINNFUL WORLD.

THIRDLY, THE YOUNG HAS TOTAL SELF CONFIDENCE. SELF ASSURANCE IS DESCRIBE IN MARY'S CONDUCT TOWARDS GOD AND ALSO TOWARDS HIS SON, FOURTHLY, THE YOUNG HAVE HOPES AND EXPECTATIONS BEYOND THEIR WILDEST DREAMS. MARY HAD ALSO HOPES AND EXPECTATIONS THAT ONLY TROUGH FAITH BECAME POSSIBLE, YET SHE WAS AWARE OF THIS WHEN SHE STATED IN MANIFIQUE THAT ALL FUTURE GENERATIONS WILL CALL HER BLESSED

FIFTH, THE YOUNG ALL LIVE WITH THE MAXIM THAT EVERYTHING IS POSSIBLE. MARY BELIEVED AND LIVED WITH TIHS GREAT PRINCIPLE: THAT WITH GOD EVERYTHING IS POSSIBLE. HERE SHE NEVER RETRACT NOR GIVE UP. SHE OFFERED THE SELF ASSURANCETHE

TOTAL CONFIDENCE, THE YOUTHFUL BELIEF THAT EVERYITHNG IS POSSIBLE TO GOD.

SIXTH, THE YOUNG ARE ALWAYS ALERT AND READY TO GO TO DO GODS WILL. THEY DO NOT HESITATE AND THIS IS THE GREAT YES THAT MARY GIVES TO GOD. ON THIS POINT SHE IS THE MAXIMUM MODEL FOR OUR ADVENT, WHEN YOU HAVE TO BE PREPARED AND ALERT FOR THE COMING OF THE LORD. MARY WAS AS READY AS EVER TO RECEIVED THE LORD.

SEVENTH, REJOYS ALL OF YOU VERY YOUNG ONES, BECAUSE HERE IS THE MYSTERY: GOD IS A CHILD AT HEART.!

SOFIA

There is great wealth in Heaven as there is great wealth on earth.

On earth there are great wealth administrators as their wisdom grow.

Money is the controlled interest of other people, with the exception of the possesor.

In Heaven, the spiritual money is the wealth that you have inside and the Virgen Mary administered the wealth of your soul, she has the right price and value of your soul.

She is the grand administrator whereby with Her, nothing is lacking for your to live an abundant life.

The spiritual money is controlled interest of the possesor, not of others people. The power of money on earth is the controlled influence and interest of other people. The power in Heaven is the soled interest of one soul.

This is why your soul is priceless and worth more than all the wealth of the earth.

Is is the power of one that makes the many be.

Our Mother full of wisdom and Sofia is her administrative name is the one who controlled the interest of the possessor of soul Virgen Mary, The Mother of God is the administrator of our spiritual wealth.

TEOTOKOS

If we believe that Jesus is God, then we must believe in the Virginity and Divinity of Mary, because She is the mother of God.

If we believe that Jesus is not God, then we can See Mary as Mary, without Virginity, without Divinity, only a woman, the mother of Jesus. The worship of Mary goes together and is congenial to our belief in our Savior . Mary is Teotokos, God bearer. The Key to Mary is the conviction that Jesus is God. The Divinity of the Son is tranmitted to the Mother . For there could be no mother without a son and no son without a mother. They simply comes in pair . and we cannot call ourselves truely brothers if we do not have a mother. Divinity is complete and complementary. Divinity cannot manifest itself without its fullness and completeness. IF there is A Son, there will be a mother, if there are brothers, by necessity there will be a mother. If there was only Son without: mother, Divinity would not be complete.

Luke 1:25-56

THE GREAT ATONEMENT

When the Lord asked Abraham to sacrifice his only son Jacob, it was a dress rehearsal of what would become reality in the life and trials of Mary.

In Abraham sacrificial rehearsal was also prophetic of What was going to happen a thousand years later. Mary was the new Abraham, obedient to God. She had the same Abraham faith that went beyond any reasonable of what God really wanted, The desire of God comes out in mystery and in uncertainty. It is reveal through trial and tribulations, through much suffering and atonement. But once the Will of God is reveal to us it is like the sun coming out after the storm, it brings to us great blessings, Great rewards of eternal life and great understanding of the mystery of existence. Yet to do the Will of God is not easy. It was not easy for Abraham who struggled with the Desire of God. Nor was it easy for Mary who find herself still a Virgin with a pregnancy that would placed her in the hands of death. Yet her "let your will be done" was all encompassing and overwhelming even for death to understand. It was a true response to the Divine mystery. It was a total acceptance that place Mary one on one with the Desire and Will of God. No Divine mystery could be again incomprehensible. No God Will could be again capricious and irrational. No Desire from God could be wrapped in mystery and be enigmatic or cruel.

Mary gave her son away in sacrifice, What Abraham could not do because God was still a Stranger, a demanding and capricious entity, He could not comprehend the irrationality of the demand. He could not transcend as Mary did, to accept the ultimate consequences of a will and desire which lies beyond the Stars and the sky. She gave up the only son she had and she place it in the altar. The sacrificial altar was Jerusalem. The knife was already the sword that had pierced her heart in two.

Jacob was Jesus not knowing his destiny until the very end. There was no testing of Abraham's faith hereabout it Was testing God's faithfulness to His promised to bring to back to life that which His own desire and mystery has killed, And God made good on his promise by resurrecting the Son of Mary. To come into conclusion what Mary knew before and after: that for God everything is possible.

In the exchanged relations between the Divine and Humanity, There has never been a more fruitful intercourse than the great atonement of Mary with God. She has conquered the alienation and estrangement of the Divine by having God be born in her by starting to say ' let your Will be done in me". From that moment on the Divine became human and human Divine.

Genesis 3: 9-15-20
Apocalysis 12: 1-6

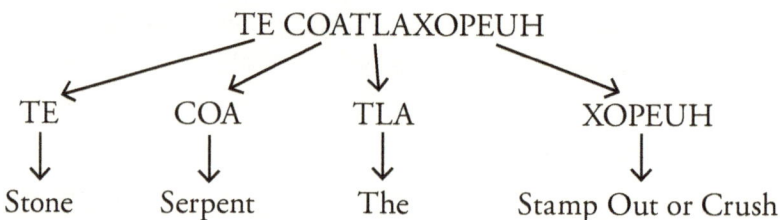

THE MARY VIRGEN NATURE

In weakness you will find strength.
In submission you will endure,
In following you will overcome the lead.
In sufferering you will understand and be king.

Because in weakness you beareth all things, believe
all things, hope all things, endure all things.
This type of philosophy is anathema to the world.
the world sides with the strong, with the breve
with the conqueror. With the unkind. But the world does
not understand that humanity has two sides to its coin;
one is female and the other male. and each one of us are
forced to chose sides, The world has chosen already its
side and the side for us. Weakness is bad, strength is the
only law it tells us. Drive yourself with love and you will
get hurt. Believe all
other male. and each one or ug are
The world has chosen already its
us. Weakness is bad, strength is the
Drive yourself with love and you will
get hurt. Believe all things, beareth all things, hope
all things and endured all things and you will be call
a fool.
Since the dawn of history to now the world has been ruled
by only one side of our humanity, the strong, masculine side.
the one that makes war in order to conquer and succed.
The One that likes greed as well as it likes violence.

the one that likes compitation as well as winning.
But this side of humanity was destained by Jesus, of Nazareth
who show to us all that the feminine side of our humanity can
be more successful than the male side. That what we call weakness
is really strength and that the world should be rule by this side
alone. That the virtues of the femine side such as
love, motherhood, hope, faith, endurance, long suffering are
the real strenght of our humanity. That they by themselves conquered
the greatest foe whether it is the Roman Empire or our own
Animial nature. As the woman conquers the man so dees this
side of humanity conquers the world and so this force was called
Christianity. But it needed a strong motif. A strong symbol of Its
nature and it was found in the Vigen mary nature. More than the
symbol of the cross where a man is dying and forsaken.. The virgen
mother of God symbol stands for the incarnate corporal of this
feminne side of humanity; the Woman. In her lies the mystery of
life; Birth! She represents one of the greatest priveleges given
to humanity; Motherhood! She is the object of Love than man bestows
through his growth stages; from, the love os the son, thru the love
or dreamer, from the love of the Lover to the love of the husband
to the love of the father, thru the love of the master.

Santa Madre De Dios Virgen Maria Guadalupana

Por

Joseph Moctezuma Rivera

Envangelio Grafico de la Nueva Creacion

Dios habla en todos lenguagje y manera de communicacion. Habla en diferentes lenguajes (lenguaje del Espiritu Santo) y se hace revelar en diferentes formas al mundo

En 1531 Dios hablo a 20 millones de indios del Nuevo Mundo, en la manera y presencia de la Virgen Maria. Plasmo en la persona de la Virgen todo el evangelio hecho en el Nuevo Testamento.

El hablo de una nueva creación espiritual de los bautisados provenientes de la Segunda Eva que proclamo San Pablo y del Segundo Adan que viene siendo Jesus.

El Senor en la Imagen de la Guadalupana, relata en grafica otra vez la creación del mundo, del sol y la luna, de la creación de las estrellas y la gran bóveda del cielo esta plasmado en la Santa Imagen de la Guadalupana.

Hablo del Mesias por venir (porque la doncella estaba en cinta). De la Reina del cielo que aparece en el cielo con corona de doce estrellas que relata el Apocalysis. De la manera en que la Virgen ve hacia el Este:donde viene el Rey (Salvador)

Hay mucho en este Evangelio Grafico de la Nueva Creacion,,poniendo a la Virgen sobre el sol y la luna y estrellas, porque viene siendo Cristo el centro del Universo creado y como dice San Pablo todas las cosas se hizo para El antes de todo los astros de cielo.

Ella es la madre sapiense, la Sabiduria que estaba con Dios antes de toda Creacion por eso cuando los Indios vieron esta Imagen, compredieron muchas cosas y secretos de Dios, atraves de la Imagen de la Guadalupana. Y su color moreno y indigina les esta diciendo a todo Indio de tes moreno que están hechos a la Imagen y semejanza de Diosl Amen.

GUADALUPANA

La Vision del Indio Juan Diego

La visión del Indio Juan Diego es que de la derrota de su
cultura sale una nueva creación que nace en la
oscuridad de la derrota, en la noche antes del amanecer
nace un modo nuevo de ser ante Dios.

No mas sacrificios humanos sino simplemete es un
ascenso al templo del Tepeyac para poder ser visto por
Dios.

No massacrificios humanos sino simplemete es un
ascenso al temple del Tepeyac para poder ser visto por
Dios.

Segundo es como Dios nos ve, no como nosotros vemos
a Dios.,

Somos de la imagen del Padre. Por eso el Padre se
representa humanamente con misericordia y simpleza
en la forma de una doncella. De tez morena que trae
confort a los derrotados indios de Mexico.

Nos trae la dignidad humana plasmada en la Imagen de
la Virgen. Que es synonimo imagen de la creacion.

La Nueva Cara de Dios es ser humano en esu Divinidad
Ser humano y divino al mismo tiempo. La Presencia de

la Virgen Guadalupana trae la experiencia del Dios mismo ante el Indio. Y le dice con su tez morena: Dios es uno como ustedes!

Su Vestuario representa lo interconeccion de toda lo creado. Toda hierba, toda piedra se vuelve dorada ante su Presencia. Transforma a todo lo creado en Divino que es la profecia como hemos de ser al final de los tiempos.

Entonces es una Imagen que empieza desde el principio de la creación hasta el final de los tiempos. Es una Imagen del cosmos mismo, del Alpha al Omega Biblico.

El Sol representa la Creación Nueva rodea al centro a una mujer joven, embarazada para dar a Iuz a un hijo a Jesus al propósito de la Creacion como lo dice San Pablo.

L a Guadalupana es Virgen y al mismo tiempo esta embarazada. La Virginidad representada la Integridad del Ser humano. Especialmente de las mujeres marginadas en un mundo machista.

Estar embarazada es plasmar en alguien tan humano y divino a la vez como es la Virgen, la Creacion completa desde el principio de Ios siglos hasta el nacimiento del Salvador.

Se nota que se cubre de estrellas. Simbolizando que Todavia de Noche para los Aztecas. Que la creación se empieza a hacer con la Voluntad Divina de Dios.

En la tradición Nanuatl de los Aztecas la luz nace en la oscuridad y es como el ave Fenix que de las cenizas nace algo nuevo.

LOS PERSONAJES (PROTOGONISTAS) DE ESTA GRAFICA NUEVA

"Los Pensamientos se ven"

Tan transluciente era la Virgen que podias ver, oir, y sentir sus pensamientos y la seguridad del conocimiento de su corazón, era como si sus pensamientos tuvieran alas que pudian volar del un estremo del universo al otro en un mismo instante.

La Virgen le pide a Juan Diego que se le contruya en el Tepeyac un "Refugio" para los derrotados por la Vida, los abandonados y victimas del destino. Los que lloran, los que sufren, las viudas, los huérfanos, los pobres los que no tienen nada.

Ella les promete: Amor, Compasion, ayuda, y protección. Les promete curalos de toda miseria, misfortuna, y sufrimiento.

Con la condición que la amen, le hablen, la buscan y que le tengan confianza en ella.

La Guadalupana es una historia viviente de un pasado histórico..

Como puede suceder que haya una "historia viva en nuestra presencia" ¿ quisas esta fue la interrogatoria que se hiciera el obispo que vio por primera vez la imagen de la Guadalupana.

Esto ensena que Dios esta aqui! Que Dios esta presente. Nuestra presencia se vuelve cósmica porque vivimos ese mismo momento también de su primera aparicision como lo vivio San Juan Diego hace 500 anios, lo vivimo hoy en este momento.

Una historia del pasado que vive en el presente y un presente que vive en la historia .

La Transformacion
De San Juan Diego

Primer encuentro con la Virgen

El primer encuentro sucede en un TIEMPO donde el corazón de San Juan Diego busca a Dios. El deseo de el de ser santo. Solo sabe que fuimos hechos a su imagen y semejanza. De Dios. Pero también sabe que la seguridad de este conocimiento esta en su corazón.. y toma su corazón y corre con el corazón en sus manos hacia Mexico.

El sabe en su corazón que Dios no quiere mas sacrificios pero ahora quiere que asienda al monte del Tepeyac (templo) para ver a Dsos. Un Dios de Misericordia y no de Sacrificios.

La otra seguridad que tiene es no ver a Dios nosotros sino que Dios nos Vea a nosotros.

Sabe también San Juan Diego que el no es Nada ante Dios reconoce lo pequeño que es el.

Su humildad hace que reciba las bendiciones de Dios altisimo su humildad era la "llave" que abre la Sabiduria de Dios y esto lo consagra para siempre. Por eso la Virgen no podia pedir esta emienda a los angeles. Solo lo podia hacer un hombre de corazón humilde como San Juan Diego.

El Lugar

Despues de ese tiempo de busquedad, se
encuentra San Juan Diego en un lugar extraño sin
embargo familiar, en un lugar que piensa San Juan
Diego que es de sus ancestros. Es allí donde se
encuetra el llamado. No esta seguro si esta en el
cielo o en otro lugar. Pero era un lugar de una
realidad tranluciente. Todo era un esplendor en
las cosas.

El lugar donde se para la Virgen Guadalupana es
un lugar de ultima Verdad. Sus pies tocan la
Verdad todo el tiempo. Ella se para sobre toda la
creado.

LA VIRGEN DESCRIBE A DIOS

En el Nican Mopohua la Virgen describe a Dios como
Dios de Verdad (Teotl), Por El que vivimos, Creador de
personas y el Dueno de lo cercano, distante. Y junto . el
Senor del Cielo y la Tierra.

La discripcion del Dueno de lo cercano es interesante,
porque simboliza lo cercano como lo eventual, lo que se
aproxima, lo que sucedera. Quiere decir que Dios es
Dueno de todo lo que nos sucede en la Vida y en la
existencia. Es Dueno de todo lo que se nos aproxima a
nosotros en la Vida. Dios es Dueno de lo junto, lo que
se une y viene a ser. Dios hace unirse el agua con el
aceite, el fuego con el agua. El cielo con la tierra. Los
opuestos son uno ante Dios. Por eso nace la luz de la
oscuridad y lo que se hace en el cielo viene a ser igual
que en la tierra.

Dios es el Creador de personas. Nadie puede ser una
persona mas que el humano y lo mas divino en la
imagen de Dios. En la persona se une todas las
caracteristicas por la cual amanos a un humano. Es un
Ser una persona

Es algo unico y singular ser una persona en la
creacion de Dios.

Es tan singular ser una persona en la creación que
hasta los poetas trantan de personaficar atraves
de lenguaje todo lo demás creado. Dicen; se
sonrien las arboles, se rien las montes, se pone
triste el mar. Bailan las o/as. Hablan las piedras.
Se sonroja la luna. Etc.

Porque no hay nada de persona en lo creado
aparte del ser humano. Pero sin embargo lo Divino
se personifica El santo Espiritu es una persona,
Dios es una persona Cristo es una persona y la
Divinidad aparece como la Virgen. Una persona
viva y divina, tan humana como uno. Esto es lo que
nos dice Dios atraves de la Virgen.

regalo que no se puede entender humanamente porque
es de procedencia Divina. Es uno de los primogénitos
regalos que Dios nos ha dado.
Dios es tambien el Proposito por lo cual vivimos. Sin
Dios no puede haber propósito en la vida. Dios es el
significado de nuestra existencia. Como dice San
Agustin: "hemos sido hechos, creados para El."
Dios es vida en ti.

Finalmente vivimos para Dios
El es el que es eterno
Nosotros solo somos un momento de su Voluntad
Antes y después Dios será de mi.
Asi la Virgen nos habla de Dios.

www.ingramcontent.com/pod-product-compliance
Lightning Source LLC
Chambersburg PA
CBHW020921140626
46545CB00015B/1197